L-1.9/p-05

Yellow Umbrella Books are published by Capstone Press
151 Good Counsel Drive, P.O. Box 669, Mankato, Minnesota 56002
http://www.capstone-press.com

Library of Congress Cataloging-in-Publication Data
Schaefer, Lola M., 1950–
    What grows from a tree?/by Lola Schaefer.
    p. cm.
    Includes index.
    ISBN 0-7368-0730-6
    1. Trees—Juvenile literature. 2. Trees—Anatomy—Juvenile literature. 3. Trees—
Physiology—Juvenile literature. [1. Trees.] I. Title.
QK475.8 .S32   2001
582.16—dc21   00-036478

Summary: Describes the parts of a tree, as well as different types of leaves, flowers, seeds, and fruit.

Editorial Credits:
Susan Evento, Managing Editor/Product Development; Elizabeth Jaffe, Senior Editor;
    Jessica Maldonado, Designer; Kimberly Danger and Heidi Schoof, Photo Researchers

Photo Credits:
Cover: Unicorn Stock Photos/Frank Pennington; Title Page: Visuals Unlimited/Bill Kamin (top left), Robert McCaw (bottom left), James P. Rowan (top right), Unicorn Stock Photos/Ted Rose (bottom right); Page 2: Terry Wild Studio/Pictor; Page 3: (clockwise from top left) Robert McCaw, Visuals Unlimited/Dennis Drenner, James P. Rowan, Unicorn Stock Photos/Marshall Prescott, J. Lotter Gurling/TOM STACK & ASSOCIATES; Page 4: Visuals Unlimited/John Sohlden (left), Unicorn Stock Photos/Steve Bourgeois (right); Page 5: Visuals Unlimited/Kjell B. Sandved, Visuals Unlimited/George Loun (inset); Page 6: Unicorn Stock Photos/B.W. Hoffmann; Page 7: Rod Planck/TOM STACK & ASSOCIATES (top left), Robert McCaw (top right), Visuals Unlimited/Bruce Clendenning (middle left), Bill Beatty (middle right), Rod Planck/TOM STACK & ASSOCIATES (bottom left), Robert McCaw (bottom right); Page 8: Unicorn Stock Photos/Karen Holsinger Mullen (top), James P. Rowan (bottom); Page 9: Photo Network/Sal Maimone; Page 10: Root Resources/Kitty Kohout (left and right); Page 11: Photo Network/Myrleen Cate (left), Unicorn Stock Photos/Marshall Prescott (right); Page 12: Visuals Unlimited/Mark E. Gibson (top left), Visuals Unlimited/Inga Spence (top right), Visuals Unlimited/John D. Cunningham (bottom left), Unicorn Stock Photos/Doris Brookes (bottom right); Page 13: Unicorn Stock Photos/Ted Rose (top), Brian Parker/TOM STACK & ASSOCIATES (bottom); Page 14: Index Stock Imagery (left), Inga Spence/TOM STACK & ASSOCIATES (top right), Visuals Unlimited/Inga Spence (bottom right); Page 15: Bill Beatty; Page 16: Index Stock Imagery

1 2 3 4 5 6 06 05 04 03 02 01

What Grows From a Tree?

By Lola Schaefer

Consulting Editor: Gail Saunders-Smith, Ph.D.
Consultants: Claudine Jellison and
Patricia Williams, Reading Recovery Teachers
Content Consultant: Jeff Gillman, Assistant Professor,
Department of Horticultural Sciences, University of Minnesota

Yellow Umbrella Books

an imprint of Capstone Press
Mankato, Minnesota

Trees are large plants.

Trees grow a trunk, roots, leaves, flowers, and seeds.

trunk

leaves

flowers

roots

seeds

Trunks are the main part of the tree. Liquid, called sap, grows in some trunks.

People gather sap from maple trees to make syrup.

Bark grows as a
hard covering
on tree trunks.
It protects the tree.

We can get cinnamon
from the bark
of this cinnamon tree.

maple

Leaves grow on trees.
Leaves make food for the tree.
Look at how different
all these leaves are.

beech

fir

palm

oak

tamarack

sassafras

Trees grow flowers.
Flowers are the colored parts
of a plant that grow seeds.

Seeds grow deep inside flowers.
When the flower petals drop,
the seeds grow bigger.

seeds

seeds

pods

Some tree seeds grow inside pods. Pods are long, hard covers that protect seeds. Seed pods fall from a tree.

Some large seeds
are called beans.
Cocoa beans can be made
into chocolate.

cocoa beans

Some seeds are nuts you can eat.
Walnuts are seeds
from a walnut tree.
Coconuts are the biggest seed
you can eat.

walnut

coconut

21011

peaches

pineapple

Some trees have a juicy food
around their seeds.
This food is called fruit.

Many kinds of fruit grow
on trees. Bananas grow on trees.
Apples grow on trees.
Even cherries grow on trees.

bananas

apples

cherries

cone

Cones are a fruit too, even
though they are not juicy.
Cones are a woody fruit.

Cones hold the seeds
of a pine tree.

Many different kinds of trees grow things we eat and use.

What do you like to eat and use that grows from a tree?

Words to Know/Index

Word Count: 244
Early-Intervention Levels: 13–16